These poems were created from the memoirs of my life. They highlight some of the significant events during my eighty-six years of life.

The many love poems were written for my wife of fifty-nine years. She passed on June 8, 2019. The love I had for her was insurmountable; the grief I felt was unbearable. I honor her with these love poems which gave me peace and solace.

This book of poems is dedicated to my wife with love, Beverly Ann Scrudato, with the support of my daughters, Joanne Barbera, Laura Kusic and inspired by my granddaughters, Jenna girl, and Gabrielle Barbera, Juliana Kusic; my grandsons, Matthew Barbera. Dr. Nicolas Barbera.

Harry was born on July 20, 1934 in Jersey City, New Jersey, to Italian immigrants. His education culminated with the graduation from James J Ferris High School in Jersey City. He volunteered for the army draft and after six months of intense training in California at Fort Ord, he was deployed to Schweinfurt, Germany for 18 months during the Cold War and achieved the rank of Specialist-3 as a training aid NCO. Shortly after arriving home, he married and had two daughters and now has five grandchildren. He attended supervisor and management courses at Rutgers University while employed by the New Jersey Turnpike Authority for 27 years as a section manager. He is an avid gardener and is known for his delicious tomatoes and figs. He now resides in the town of Secaucus, New Jersey, for the past 50 years.

This book was inspired by my daughters Joanne Barbera and Laura Kusic and my five grandchildren Dr. Nicolas Barbera, Jenna Barbera, Matthew Barbera, Gabrielle Barbera and Juliana Kusic. I dedicate this book to the love of my life, my wife of 60 years Beverly Ann Scrudato.

Harry Scrudato

Love Poems from the Heart

AUSTIN MACAULEY PUBLISHERS™

LONDON • CAMBRIDGE • NEW YORK • SHARJAH

Ordering Information
Quantity sales: Special discounts are available on quantity purchases by corporations, associations, and others. For details, contact the publisher at the address below.

Publisher's Cataloging-in-Publication data
Scrudato, Harry
Love Poems from the Heart

ISBN 9781638297116 (Paperback)
ISBN 9781638297123 (e-Pub e-book)

Library of Congress Control Number: 2022923662

www.austinmacauley.com/us

First Published 2023
Austin Macauley Publishers LLC
40 Wall Street, 33rd Floor, Suite 3302
New York, NY 10005
USA

mail-usa@austinmacauley.com
+1 (646) 5125767

I would like to thank Joanne Barbera, Laura Kusic and Dr. Nicolas Barbera for their patience, time and effort in helping to make this book a reality.

Soliloquy of Love

The time was drawing near, I sat by her bedside, no words were spoken, our eyes had met in the valley of love. I held her hand tightly, a sweet kiss on the lips, she was now entering uncharted waters, her eyes closed for the last time, as I watched a tear float from a closed eye. I whispered in her ear, I am with you, I felt her hand tightly grasping mine, moments later, her hand went limp and with her all my tomorrows had gone.

Tonight before bedtime, tell someone you love them.

We don't cry because it's over, we smile because it happened.

Dr. Suess.

The Being of Me

Poems, like love letters written in the sand, cannot be taken away by the ripples of a wave.

Family, the hub of all life. Family means to share, to love, to forgive. We stand together, love as one, if one had misfortune, we all felt the pain. One who is without family is without love; it is the meaning of life.

We all start in the same place, we all end in the same place, it is in the middle that counts.

Some of the following lines were taken from the song. Where do you start?

Music by Johnny Mandel, Lyrics by Marilyn and Alan Bergman.

The true story of my love was written in the form of poetry.

Where do you start? How do you separate the present from the past?

All the dreams and pictures that all came true.

Our lives were tangled like the branches of a vine that intertwined.

How do you deal with the things you thought would last?

With bits of memories scattered here and there.

I look around and don't know where to start.

When you read these poems of love, you will be looking into the being me.

Her demise brought anger, sorrow, and tears, these many poems of love gave me peace. Other poems were of family and events.

Section One
Love Poems from the Heart

A Marriage Made in Heaven

You said you would always love me,
you said you would always care.
When you left me, my heart was torn in two,
just thinking about you.

Now who will remember my birthday?
Who will kiss me goodnight?
And when I sometimes falter,
You were always there, to show me the light.

I lie awake in bed each night,
waiting for the morning air.
My days are long and lonely,
I hide from my despair.

One day we'll be together again,
and when that day comes, our hearts will be one.
The months go by and yet, I still feel the anger there as,
I am here, and she is there.

One day we'll be together again,
Hand in hand with God, once again.

Life's Dreams

Years have come and gone,
and left me old and gray.
Alone in my thoughts,
each and every day.

My life is but a dream,
the dreams of yesterday.
The dreams of gaiety and youth,
when we were young forever yesterday.

She left me with tears and sorrow,
as life is funny that way.
The Mona Lisa smile,
I dream of each and every day.

Life of dreams together,
hearts full of love.
The tenderness of her kiss,
were dreams of yesterday's wish.

The days go by are long and blue,
nights are sadness too.
Father time cannot erase,
my love for you.

Enchanting Love

The electricity in the air,
showed me how much she cared,
the mood was right,
ready for our lite.

Tender kiss on the lips,
to start an exciting trip,
like honey from a bee,
her soft hands upon me.

To continue our flight,
our rapture felt right,
we started to reach the height,
we moved on to our delight.

From way up on high,
we shared our free fall from the sky,
it lasted forever, and yet,
It was faster than ever.

A word was not spoken,
we were filled with emotions,
quiet as a mouse,
our love has filled the house.

The music had ended,
we went on with our day,
it was a part of our love,
in our lives for a day.

When We Were Young

When We Were Young,
we didn't have a care,
our spirits were as free as the air.
When We Were Young.

As time went on,
our bodies grew,
and our minds did too.
When We Were Young.

Our teenage years
were full of smiles and tears,
and yet our happy days were full of cheers.
When We Were Young.

As we grew older, waiting for our love,
the days were long and lonely,
our love may never come.
When We Were Young.

In our years of grey,
waiting on their kids,
still our hearts we're young,
When We Were Young.

The golden years are here,
We look back on the years,
the empty nest appears with sadness and tears,
when we were young forever yesterday.

All I See Is You

In all those many years together,
everything I see, reminds me of you.
The simple touch of your hand in mine,
happy days when we went to dine.

Music that we listened to,
your head resting on my shoulder,
your tender lips upon mine,
these things remind me of you.

Scattered pictures of yesterday,
the days we left behind.
our traveling days of yesteryear,
all the places we held dear.

Sunny Italy, with days of song and wine,
are memories in my mind.
My memories of the past,
all I see is you.
The dreams which all came true,
how blessed I was to be with you.

Many Years Ago

Many years ago,
when we were carefree and young,
there was sunlight in your eyes,
how cheerful we were then.

My years were full of gaiety and you,
the morning sunshine of our happy youth,
in my heart I will always remember,
olden days of carefree youth with you.

In the evening, with moonlight in your eyes.
our love grew stronger,
like branches on a vine,
sweet as vintage wine.

Her pixie black hair turn to gray
she suddenly passed away.
Day by day I looked for a way,
all the years had fade away,
I don't see me in her eyes as before.

Illusion

I see her walking through the door,
bright and smiling, as before.
I see her standing in the light,
her green eyes shining bright.

As our hearts had met,
a word was not spoken,
she kissed me on the cheek,
with love and devotion.

A picture to behold, small talk of the day,
we sat down to dine, as she sipped her wine.
I was fortunate to have her mine,
at least for a period of time.

Evening had come with music she liked,
phantom of the Opera, music of the night.
Evening had ended, she changed for bed,
retired for the night, she was a beautiful sight.

With my eyes wide open
I dreamed of dreams of yesterday,
tried to find a better way to say,
I love you.

Lying in bed to hold her tight,
in the middle of the night,
when the mood was right,
the magic had gone, the illusion was there,
I had no one to share.

The Hurt Never Stops

It's been a year since you left,
summer has come and gone,
fall leaves turn to gold,
blustery winters are cold,
back to the spring,
when she left me.

Four seasons in my mind,
I think of the times she was mine.
Summer time when we went to the beach,
sat in the yard, without a word,
hearing the love song of a bird.

Fall came, the leaves had turned,
her hair tied in a green ribbon reflecting her eyes,
chill of the autumn breeze,
walked along with a hug and a squeeze.

The winter arrives with snow on the ground.
She wears her boots, a scarf and a crown.
She was my queen of the May, on that winter day.

With spring in the air, the warm air arrives.
The crocus pokes out of the ground,
the daffodils quickly follow around,
And yet, she was nowhere to be found.

We loved when alive,
we shared our hearts and our minds
for when she is gone, there's only a memory in mind.
There is no tomorrow, tomorrow is only borrowed.

Old Man's Lament

My life as I knew it before
is no longer here anymore.
I cannot put my head on her shoulder,
as I'm getting older.
All those years disappear,
never more to appear.

I look at life so different now,
as that was then, and now is now.
The simple things we did together,
which made our lives enchanting,
those times I took for granted.

My eyes stare in space,
seeing only her face.
I hear her voice echoed in my mind,
I feel her hand upon mine,
this is in the corner of my mind.

My days are all a new,
I learned to live my life without you.
I'm all alone in the morning,
I sit alone with no one to share, playing solitaire.

The noon day sun is not any fun.
The emptiness of the day
makes my life dull and gray.

I speak words aloud,
with no one to here,
you make good friends that way,
with no one to fear.

Dusk arrives at the end of the day.
I read a book without the words,
and listen to the song of a bird.
The midnight moon appears,
I end my day with sadness and tears.

I lie awake in bed each night,
with eyes wide open, I sleep not a wink,
start all over and try not to think.
I wake up at dawn, as light appears,
I fear the grim reaper may be near,
another day in the past many years.

Love's Eternal

Dedicated with love to my three granddaughters: Jenna Barbera, Gabrielle
Barbera and Juliana Kusic

The first time I saw her,
my heart skipped a beat.
Her smiling eyes had captured me
I was forever in love.

With each passing day,
she was happy and gay.
She never said I was in the way.

Not a day went by,
she always hug me with a sigh,
I saw my reflection in her eyes.

The weeks had passed,
I thought her love would never last.
I asked myself, why was I so lucky,
to have you in my pass.
The months passed into years,
with happiness and cheers.

My heart is very weak,
I kissed her on the cheek,
she embrace me and held my tight,
tears in her eyes, love in her heart,
never to depart. I love you, Pop, as love is eternal.

Final Goodbye

We said goodbye so many times before,
went to buy a dress, I said goodbye.
She always came home as before,
the movies with a friend I said goodbye,
greeted her home as before.

Through our lives we said goodbye many times before,
final goodbye is not like before.
The day came, she gave her last confession.

Sat at her bedside my heart was broken,
afraid to close my eyes,
afraid that I'll find, she'll be gone.
Held her hand with love and devotion,
kissed her on the lips, eyes opened wide.
Uncontrollable tears in my eyes.

I held her face, a tender embrace,
the sweet look on her face will never be erased.
With no sound, her lips said I love you so,
I whispered in her ear, I'll never let you go.
Closed her eyes, never more to rise.
We said our final goodbyes.

Dream

My life is but a dream,
eyes wide open I'm dreaming,
I dream through the day,
hoping she'll come my way.

I can't wait to sleep at night,
waiting for the morning light,
praying she'll be there as before.
With coffee in hand, coming through the door,
wake up lazy bones, there are many chores.

Each day is the same as the last,
I'm daydreaming through the day,
hoping she would come my way,
I live my days in a haze,
in so many many ways.

I pinch myself to see if I'm alive,
won't give up or compromise.
Praying for a miracle.
Deep inside I know will never come,
until the final day when we are one.

Together Again

Don't cry for me my children,
I'm now happy at rest.
The day has come will be together as one
I'm happy with my new bride,
like we first started side-by-side.

She said she would wait,
be standing at the gate.
Will kiss as before,
as we walk through the door.

A new adventure will start,
like we first met.
Our dreams came true,
when we first said, I do.

Will walk through the gates,
in the heavens above.
We'll love as before,
this time we'll be, forever more.

A Little Bit of Heaven

The day you wore white,
you were so beautiful and bright,
you're heart full of love,
singing the song of a dove.

Your lovely smile said I do,
I could not take my eyes off of you.
You were the picture of charm,
As you tightly held my arm.

With dreams in our hearts,
we were ready to depart.
Our new life had been charted,
a new beginning had started.

With a new life of our own.
We set a course for the unknown.
Many years had passed,
each year was better than the last.

The day the Grim Reaper appeared,
my heart was full of anguish and tears,
she look like the first day we met,
with heaven in her eyes, I can never forget.

Can't Let Go

Much time has passed,
I still love you so,
time and time again,
I can't let you go.

Other loves may come my way,
the feeling is not that way,
I only have feelings for one,
it cannot be undone.

The love we had was only ours,
our love was as strong as the sun.
Only fools would dare to depart,
The devil cannot shade our hearts.

Some people say, go on with your life,
you can always take another.
I cannot go on with the game of life,
she will always be my wife.

Prisoner

Our beautiful marriage had ended,
she left for the great beyond.
No one can prepare you
for the love that's left behind.

I live in the shadows of my mine,
for what I left behind.
I eat my meals alone each day,
only to keep the sickness away.

There are no bars on my windows,
nor locks on the doors,
not the home I knew before.
No place to go, I can't ignore.

In the courtroom of life,
what was I punished for?
I am a prisoner of sort,
with no recourse.

The Feeling of Love

What it means to me to say I love you,
what it means to me to say I care.
Your happy smile when you're around me,
makes me feel how much I really care.

When I say I love you, it's not a word or two,
it's the feeling in my heart that makes it true.
When you're around me, the feeling never ends.
It's that feeling that begins and ends with you.

The cute way you toss your rhymes about,
that Mona Lisa smile there's no doubt.
The rhythm in my heart whenever I think of you,
that's the love I feel for you.

The feeling I have never comes and goes,
it's always here when you're are near.
That's what it means to me when I say I love you so,
that's the feeling I will never let you go.

Hard to Explain

It's so hard to explain,
the love that I had,
not so long ago.
The quiet smile on her face,
cannot be replaced,
in the whole human race.

The love in my heart,
since we are apart,
simply will never depart.
Makes my blood pressure rise.
I realize all the love,
for her, deep inside.

It is so hard to explain,
I write these words with pain.
When the music stopped,
my heart just dropped.

I am not the same person I was before,
all my love went out the door.
I am not the same guy I was before,
I am listless and dull, my brain is a hull.

She was the spark that made me fly.
Why did she have to die?
The thrill in my life is gone.
It's very difficult to carry on.
There are no words to be spoken.
I remember the past like poetry in motion.

Time goes on, it is what it is,
you cannot change the past.
You go on with your life,
there is nothing more you can do,
the true picture comes into view.

Irish Rose

The sun was shining brightly the day I saw her in the park.
My heart skipped a beat or two, the time I first saw you.

Your green eyes came into view, our hearts did too.
The smell of roses fill the air,
I first met my wild Irish rose there.

She was a picture of heaven, a sight to behold;
my heavenly pot of gold.
It was the day we were married, our hearts became one.

The years went by quickly, in a way.
We woke up one morning, we were silver and gray,
when the good Lord came her way.
She left with a smile, said she would wait at the gate,
no matter how long it would take, she said she would wait.

Midnight Summer's Dream

In the small of the night, I lie awake in my flight,
I hear the raging quiet in the forest of the night.
The soft wind that blow her name about,
clouds that gather for the soft rain throughout
that makes the morning dew, reminds me of you.

The sweet morning smell of the woodland area,
small animals of the night come alive in the morning light.
Turns her head and holds me tight,
start of our day she made the morning bright.

Mid-morning sun peers through the trees below.
A water stream's from the mountain snow,
slide like a snake to the lake below.
The quiet demeanor of her smile,
like the quiet lake, a contented child.

Noontime brings the heat of the day,
lovely and warm when we had our way.
Like the trees of the forest grow strong from the sun,
the strength you gave me when we were one.

The shade eclipsed the middle of the day,
quiet and serene made the forest that way.
Like the animals in repose from the work of the day,
she was my delight each day.

Darkness fell on the forest below,
trees gather their strength of the day.
It's time to put the forest away.
We relaxed for a time, ready to rest for the night.
I abruptly awaken, I went alone in the night.

When Is Enough Enough

All these many months have passed,
I continue to feel the hurt deep inside.
Will this ache ever depart?

I remember the love from yesterday,
a love that will never go away.
I wait for the day I can dream without a tear, dream of love as before.
To love as though you are here forever more.

With magic in the air, I hold you tightly,
feeling your sweet lips upon mine.
When will be the day?
When is enough, enough?
I will wait till the cows come home to play.

Till Death Do Us Part

(Birthday Wishes)

Till death do us part were the words that were spoken 59 years and 2 days ago, when we were joined together as one.

It has been over 14 months since she passed. I still feel the ache in my heart. Till death do us part are only words that were spoken and were untrue, as death did not do us part.

That day when we were joined together as one continues throughout eternity.

When it is time for my last confession, we will once again be joined as one, until then, my darling, I wish you a very happy birthday.

My Deepest Love, Harry

Mona Lisa Smile

I remember the Mona Lisa smile, though you are gone.
The smile that lights my way.
The flower of my dreams
that brings the morning dew.
I look into your eyes; I see all the love you gave to me.
All the happiness that love can be which all came true.

The sunlight in your smile,
this is what you mean to me, this is all I see.
Now that you are gone,
I will be remembering,
all the joy you brought to me,
with that Mona Lisa smile.

Wait for Me

I'm alone in the darkness,
there is no one to guide me.
In the shadow of my thoughts, I would have to go where life leads me.

With no one beside me, no one to guide me, I wait in the wilderness of my
heart.

I find myself alone and in despair.
I journey through life in sorrow.
With the help of time, the darkness will hide me; with you by my side, we'll
find a new way.
I realize the old days of fun and laughter are over.
The new day will only come when I come to you. I'll have someone who
needs me. I can go where destiny leads me.
I looked at the blue sky above, I see your smiling face. Look into my eyes,
you will see the spark that lights a star. Wait for me.

Section Two
Memoirs in My Mind

Coronavirus

The theaters are empty,
the restaurants too.
The quaint shops are closed,
the malls are empty too.

With masks on our face,
we stand six feet apart,
we dare not touch.
We wait for the devil to depart.

The schools are deserted,
the streets are too,
few cars on the roadway,
makes our minds empty too.

No homework to do,
their brains in despair,
We fear the dreaded disease may be there.
We pray and hope, not beyond repair.

They watch TV and read good books,
as there's no place to go.
Spirits are low with no get up and go.
Coronavirus is in town lurking around.

It's scary as hell, with hope in our heart,
a dream will come true, we'll be through with you.
When that day comes,
good riddance, goodbye to you.

We dream of dreams of yesterday,
when we were happy and gay.
Now the coronavirus is in our way,
the day will come we'll have our way,
when this dreaded disease is at bay.

The Sickness Continues

If the music starts
and it plays your song
loud and clear, beware
The Big "C" may be there.

If it arrives
with a nasty look,
hate in his heart,
and meanness in its eyes,
you must stand strong
or it will never depart.

With the stoutness of heart
and strength in your soul,
you must fight to conquer,
you must be bold.

As the months go by
the treatments are long.
The unbearable hate
that you bear in your soul.

There may be a setback or two
waiting for you.
You cannot let this monster
take charge of you.

The day will come
when the treatments will end,
you will be healthy again.
With God on your side,
this misery will end.

It did not happen that way,
it was heartbreaking to see.
It now spread to the brain,
her body was racked with pain.

As the end was near,
she gave me a smile and a kiss,
she closed her eyes and was gone.
I saw the flower in my heart disappear,
she saw the good Lord appear.

The anguish was there like never before,
my love had gone through the door,
never to return anymore.

I now have the photographs
of memories gone bye.
She was pretty as a picture
so healthy and new.
These are the memories I have of you.

The once beautiful girl I knew
who made my life young and new
is no longer in view.
I live my life in pain,
nevermore to return.

Teachers

Dedicated to my daughter: Laura Scrudato Kusic

The value of school teachers are taken for granted.
They are maligned, overpaid, vacation days, every way. Grammar level,
children learn the three 'R's.
It was no accident, children could read, the effort made by teachers, made this,
indeed.

Their minds are developed, they learn how to think,
this does not happen with a wink.
The hardworking teachers are at work
to teach the children every day of the week.

Discipline is needed as all children must have,
homework is needed in the lab.
The teachers spend hours correcting their work,
no one sees how long they work.

They continue in high school with the background they need.
They prep for college with the subjects they need,
with their teacher there to guide them along.
In a flash of a light they continue their flight.

The next phases is college with stars in their eyes,
some become teachers and hope for the best.
Their vocations are blessed, to go on to teach the rest.

The cycle continues, the new teachers are there,
nervous and new, they realize the children are too.
As time goes by, they understand it's not fun and games.
It's hard work to get into their brains.

Smart people know teachers take a nasty blow.
The respect they deserve does not always show.
For without the teachers at hand,
there would be no doctors, nurses, or preaches on hand,
who would mend our souls, who would keep us alive,
if no teachers survived.

A Time to Live and
a Time to Die

Everyone gets their turn in the box.
Does not matter how much you use botox.
No one is exempt from the magic of death,
we all end up at a six foot depth.

There are no do-overs in life.
Everyone goes around only once.
Riches cannot bring an extension of life.
You may hold the highest office in the land,
when your number's up, it only brings you a band.
The doctor who keeps you well and alive,
cannot keep from going, no matter how he tries.

There's a box made for everyone.
It's your turn when you receive the key.
There are those who try to beat the system.
No one has the smarts nor the wisdom.
There are those who make a duplicate key,
some build a side pocket for their money.
We all end in the same place, with the Easter bunny.

A House Is Not a Home

A house is made of brick and mortar, wood and stone,
without a heart it cannot stand alone.
It takes laughter and fun, sadness and tears,
makes a house a home, to make the rainbows appear.

The babe cries in the middle of the night.
She reaches for the light, to get the babes delight,
with love in her heart, and the babe in her arms,
she prays this magic will never depart.

The kids scamper around and play with their toys,
they move about with all the noise.
Soon the school days appear,
within a whim your school days will disappear.

The young babes are now in college as life goes on.
Their bodies have grown and their minds have to,
with fun in their hearts, their thoughts on the future.
Their lives are happy and fruitful too.

Now they are married with kids of their own,
the cycle continues with babies of their own.
Time goes by, a house of their own,
with love in their heart, makes a house a home.

Marie

Written for my dear friend, Marie Kusic

The story of a girl called Marie.
Pretty and sassy as she could be.
As a young girl, she found her man,
a man named Stan.

They courted for a while as young couples do,
then came the war, World War II.
She felt empty inside as you can guess,
as Stan joined the fight and left.

After three years in the Rhineland,
Stan came home to the mainland.
Laughter and tears, endeared again.
They charted a course together again.
The wedding date was set, off they went.
With love in their hearts, never to depart.
Pretty as a picture, dreams of the future,
it didn't take long as four boys came along.

Paul, Gregory, Rocky and Jeff,
all tall and handsome as anyone could get.
Big and strong, was proud of her boys,
she kept them in line, they grew up fine.

Time has passed with happiness and tears.
Many years later, the empty nest appeared.
Stan had passed, with faith in God.
She survived.

At ninety-six, eyeing one hundred six,
Marie looks back at her wedding pics.
With memories gone by,
Perky and strong, she forges along.

She remembers the day, her children at play.
Now she sees her grandchildren at play.
How lucky she feels to be a part of their life,
when Stan made her his wife.

The story ends, one eye on the future.
One eye on the past,
enjoying the days as they last.

Nifty Fifties

Our high school years have come and gone,
when the boys wore their collars up,
and they walked to a beat of a silent drum.
The girls wore their skirts ankle high,
they Swaggart along as they came strolling by.

Saturday night dances were cool and great.
They danced the swing with their date.
Big bands going out, rock and roll came in with a spin,
kids loved the sound, as a new era was to begin.

It was a great life, no cares, no worries, just fun,
we lived our life as though it would never end,
we were in the sunshine of our happy youth,
not knowing the truth, it would soon end.

The gay days of high school were over, it was time to leave, our senior year
with sadness and tears. The years pass with the tide, they do not last, slow
down, enjoy the ride.

The Journey

The journey through life is the essence of our being; it is only a passage of which we travel that makes us who we are. The choices we make at the start of our journey until the last confession, shapes our character. During the journey, the decisions we make along the way can never be reversed, you alone can only choose. Most of the decisions we make in life are simple. It is a matter of right and wrong, this decision is easy to make, if you make the wrong decision it will come back to haunt you at the end, the other few decisions will be a matter of faith.

As we travel on the highway of life, we can look back in our rear-view mirror on how it shaped our lives. The exits which we may have taken may have been wrong. There are no U-turns on the highway of life. Map out your course and take the right road, enjoy.

From the Womb to the Tomb

When the big show starts,
from the very beginning,
so shiny and new,
the new world takes hold of you.

A baby in arms,
feeling of your mother's charm,
love that you feel, is ever so real.
Your eyes open wide,
the new world comes alive.

From infant to toddler,
Mom by your side,
learn to walk and speak.
The process is long and unique.
Each day takes a year,
each year, a new frontier,

School days appear,
wonder in your eyes,
what each day would comprise,
a new day, a surprise.
As a teenager, one year equals ten,
an eternity back then,
as years come in a blink,
and gone in a wink.

Now we are parents,
with children of our own.
They grow up so fast,
we try to slow up, to make it last.

Grandparents at last,
we enjoy the fruits of the past,
the years go by,
now it's our turn to die.

If the world was run
by the toddlers in command,
there would be no wars,
we would all understand.
We'd live our lives as planned.

The Definition of a Mother

Definition of the word mother,
Dictionary version, Woman in relation to a child.

True definition,
The Woman who brings you into the world;
when you're a child, the person who is there,
when you're in need of care.

The Teacher, from whom you learn,
one who is truly concerned.

The Doctor, who heals you when you're sick.
When you call, she is very quick.
The Preacher, when you're in need,
trying times arrive, keeps your heart and soul alive.

The Attorney, always within the law, as time began,
gives you advice as only a mother can.

The Nurse, when you are sick she's up all night,
with fright, waiting for the morning light.

The Cook, she prepares your food, hoping you'll like,
to keep you healthy and bright.

The Housekeeper, washes your clothes and cleans your house, make sure you
have a clean blouse.

I'm sure you get the picture now,
we must make room for other definition to define,
mother is not the only word in the book,
other words need a look.

There Are So Many Ways to Love

I love that Broadway play,
love this beautiful day,
love the day you came my way.

Sweet love of holding your child.
The time they learned to laugh and smile.
The emotion you have when she begins to speak,
love for the child that makes you weak.

The excitement of your first love.
Courtship which makes two different worlds one,
the romance which was never undone.

There are many different shades of love,
the love of your mother,
your sister, or your brother.
The shades of love are endless and different,
each shade is lovely and magnificent.

A Letter for Mom

Mom, with the help of Rocky and Sue, we bring you a gift to show that we are always with you.

A plaque was completed with loving hands by Laura and Jeff, a thing of beauty which we left.

The sand came from Joanne & Tony's shore place, for
the plaque to be embedded by your place.

A poem was inspired by your grandchildren from the love they feel for you.

They gave me the inspiration to write the words I leave for you,
until we meet again.

I leave this poem to give you comfort and peace,
for when we meet again in heaven, we both will have peace.

Your loving husband.

Nicolas; the Titanium Man

I saw you grow from a toddler to a man,
strong as uranium, the titanium man.
As a young boy, looking at the world
with wonderment and emotion,
so eager to learn, to fill your devotion.

Learned of the dinosaurs of years gone by,
you would teach the teachers of history gone by,
she was amazed at your skill how you filled the bill,
someday I will read about you,
when you reach the top of the hill.

The world at your doorstep you continued to climb,
Your school days gone by, it was only a matter of time.
Your chemical engineering degree in hand,
now your PhD in command.

I wait for the day will take a trip to Norway,
the many accomplishments you did your way,
you will be in the Garden of Eden.

If I am not here when that day comes,
from the heavens above I'll watch with Grandma when you are the one.

Make Believe

I'm living in the world of make believe,
my heart is empty and blue,
all I do is think of you.
I remember the early days gone by,
when we were happy and new.
I now see a world that is black and blue.

I pretend that you're with me to keep my spirits high,
no matter how much I try,
it does not work when you said goodbye.

In times gone by, I remember seeing the world in your eyes,
you made my hopes and dreams come true.
I'm now living in a world where children do,
a fairy land where no dreams come true.

I see my days in a haze, where all others see the light,
I am bubbly and spry when I see my children come by,
they see me happy and gay, but it's not that way,
I live my life in a lie each and every day.

Land of make believe are for children at play.
When grown-ups play the game, it's not that way.
It's visions of grief, visions of sorrow,
your heart has been pierced by a poison arrow.

You live life in despair, there's no true happiness there.
Your family comes by, you pretend to be happy and gay,
stay strong with a smile on your face, till the end of the day.

My life is but a dream,
a dream of nightmares and horrors.
I see her sweet face, only to see it erased.
The horror continues until the morning break.

I wake up to another day of make believe.
Another day I continued to deceive,
another place in the land of make believe.

Matthew—Renaissance Man

Like the Phantom he roams,
you never know if he's home.
He comes and he goes,
you never know when he shows.

He's a man of all seasons,
for this he has many reasons.
His heart is warm as the sun,
you see why he is the one.

He can change at a glance,
make you feel good in advance,
sits down and listens,
and yet, be in command.

He has a way with the ladies,
can put them at ease,
he now has a lady, his main squeeze.

He's a modern day renaissance man,
he has the unique ability to get things done,
now you know, he is the one.

His life goes on, you never know where he'll be,
he'll come without warning and stay till morning.
Never know where he roams.

He'll be there in a flash if you're in need,
help you in any way indeed.
With his heart in his hand.
He is totally in command,
the Renaissance Man.

The Feeling of Love

What it means to me to say I love you,
what it means to me to say I care.
Your happy smile when you're around me
makes me feel how much I really care.

When I say I love you, it's not a word or two,
it's the feeling in my heart that makes it true.
When you're around me, the feeling never ends.
It's that feeling that begins and ends with you.

The cute way you toss your rhymes about.
That Mona Lisa smile there's no doubt.
The rhythm in my heart whenever I think of you.
That's the love I feel for you.

The feeling I have never comes and goes,
it's always here when you're are near.
That's what it means to me when I say I love you so.
That's the feeling I will never let you go.

My Daughter's, the Sisters

They gave us ten days to say goodbye,
they told my daughters and I.
We were totally taken by surprise.
How suddenly we would lose our prize.

In our hearts, she made the sunrise,
for this we never realized,
we took for granted what was before our eyes.

The first day we were told, we had a group cry.
A drink in hand, they took command.
With their husbands support,
arrangements were made to bring her home,
with the only loves she had ever known.

Day and night they made her comfortable and warm.
They had taking care of her every need,
watched over me like a sick puppy indeed.

Within those ten days, I was taking sick with the heart.
They put me to bed each night, like a babe in arms.
They took care of me, afraid now two might depart.

The end was near, tired and extended,
with stoutness of heart, they would never surrender.
The day came when she was put to rest.
We knew the day would come,
but still unprepared for the outcome.
Arrangements had to be made to prepare her for her final rest.

The chores were taken by the sisters.
Emotions in hand they continued on with love and devotion.

Now my daughter's make the sun rise,
I don't take for granted what is before my eyes.
I thank the good lord that now I realize.

Crisis

It was a scary and worried time.
A letter arrived from the military,
there's a crisis at hand,
one more year is needed,
to fill my military demand.

The Cuban missile crisis arrived,
with a bang and a holler,
a new war may be here,
as a crisis is near.

This war would not be like before,
It would annihilate us all,
on both sides of the wall.
Words were spoken,
on both sides of the fence,
we must make peace, at no expense.

I had two children at hand,
I must think of their need,
and yet, if the big show started,
there would be no need.

The talks must continue,
a way must be found.
Level heads must prevail,
not to destroy the holy grail.

The talks were in progress,
as the world was in fright,
each side must save face,
as the leaders must be right.

For the grace of God, they found a way,
to bring us peace for one more day.
If the curtain went up,
the world could be blackened…
who knows what could have happened.

The cold war continues with words,
and not deeds.
At least they answered our immediate needs.

The Sickness Continues

If the music starts
and it plays your song
loud and clear, beware
The Big "C "maybe there.

If it arrives
with a nasty look
hate in his heart
and meanness in its eyes,
you must stand strong,
or it will never depart.

With stoutness of heart
and strength in your soul,
you must fight to conquer,
you must be bold.

As the months go by
the treatments are long.
The unbearable hate
that you bear in your soul.

There may be a set back or two
waiting for you.
you cannot let this monster
take charge of you.

The day will come
when the treatments will end.
You will be healthy again.
With God on your side
this misery will end.

I Remember

There was a time I remember, we were children at play, in the sunshine of a happy way. We played City Street games, stickball, football made of a rolled-up newspaper, kick the can, Johnny on a pony. There were other made up games that kids could play on city streets.

It was December 7, 1941, Sunday morning, the church bells were ringing, the look of fright on the faces of morning church worshippers. At seven years old, I had no idea what was going on.

I surmised it was bad.

The following poem was created through the eyes of a seven year old boy.

I Remember

I felt alone and frightened,
there was no place to turn,
children were to be seen and not heard.

I saw my mom crying when her son went to war.
She was weak from horror, as she fell to the floor.
She was not the same mom as I knew before,
As the weeks had passed, we were losing the war.
As the radio gave us news of the war,
every day was worse than before.

Each night, the siren alarm would sound,
each home would pull the curtains tight,
to keep out the light.

Time went on, came the Battle of Midway,
now we would have it our way.
I still did not realize what was in store for the day.

I cried myself to sleep each night,
not knowing if everything would be alright.
There was rationing of food a shortage of all,
we did what we did for the benefit of all.
The kids collected paper, rags and metal for the fight.
The effort was made each day and every night.
The years had passed, the mood got lite,
for now we were winning the fight.

Five years had passed, the war was over.
My brother came home to roses and clover.
The stranger was home I was soon to know,
Learned to love my new brother so.

Intangible Love

Intangible love within your soul,
is what makes us whole,
a lovely thing to behold.
You may think with your brain,
it takes a heart to explain.

Sadness comes by,
makes a tear in your eye.
When anger comes into play,
your day is in disarray,
it's the heart in your soul,
that keeps you in control.

When you see your love,
with a glow in her eye,
kiss on the lips, cannot be dismissed.
Excitement cannot be denied.
Intangible heart opens inside.

Intangible heart cannot be touched,
for the heart is not there,
invisible to the eye, cannot be seen.
Intangible heart is within you, being.
Intangible heart,
you can wish upon a star,
can dream to the extreme,
you can reach for the moon,
and catch a star.
No one will know who you are.

Dreams and hopes are endless.
Invisible heart is your secret.
If someone knows,
it is no longer a secret.
You go on with life,
you're never be alone,
you will always have something to own.

Left on the Street
Corner Alone

It was an early September morning,
I was suddenly awakened from bed,
with sleep in my eyes, I was surprised,
today was the day I did not realize.

At five years old, my first day at school,
I slowly got dressed, short pants was the rule.
I had my egg for the day, Mom was funny that way.
She rushed me along, my sister by my side.
She took my hand, and we walked side-by-side.

The seven-year-old girl and I briskly walked to school.
We arrived so early,
I thought she had to open the gate to the school.
There was no one around, I was so scared,
I did not make a sound.

She left the young boy on the corner alone.
Do not fret the teacher will soon come from home,
alone on the corner, alone in my thoughts,
I was excited and scared, what would soon come to bear.

It seems like a year when the teacher appeared.
The parents assembled with their kids in hand.
We were taken to class, marching hand-in-hand.
There was a table with sand,
I thought I could play, but it was not that way.

A boy much bigger than I, had tears in his eyes.
I asked, why so sad, he replied,
my shoe is untied, I am unable to tie.
I tied his shoe, his sadness stopped.
That time on, we were friends for life,
even after he got a wife.

Empty House

(No one can prepare you for an Empty house.)

It's been awhile since she left me,
I still feel empty inside,
the silence in the air,
puts your mood in despair.

I arise in the early mmourning,
to the silence of a cloudy morning.
Since she went away, the house is cold and gray,
no amount of heat can take that away.

I look around the room,
all I see is gloom.
With memories scattered here and there,
the pictures that we shared, made me aware.

In my mind, I see her there,
sitting in her chair,
our house was full of love,
with music in the air.

Our house is empty now,
no laughter in the air,
silence is hard to bear, with no one to share.

Nine Eleven

As she watched in the sky,
a tear came to her eye,
she could not stand by.
The smoke filled the sky.

She went to the Jersey pier,
where all the boats appeared.
She became a volunteer.

They filled private boats with water,
to bring to the New York side.
She was one of many to hand out water
to the people, to help restore order.

They filled the boats with folks,
to bring to the Jersey side.
They could not understand,
they felt they were going to die.

She continued the work till evening.
Came home exhausted and tired,
clothes full of dust and debris.
She rested her head upon me.
I asked her where she had been,
I don't know where to begin.
She told me, many people in a daze,
I helped them in many ways.

I was angry as hell,
she may have been hurt.
With her Mona Lisa smile on her face,
I had to go, it was my place.

A number of years later,
a growth appeared on her skin,
the melanoma had spread within.

Goodbye, I love you,
with a sweet kiss on the lips.
I lost my love unprepared,
which can never be repaired.

The anguish was there like never before,
my love had gone through the door,
never to return anymore.

I remember when we walked side-by-side.
She was pretty as a picture, so healthy and new.
Now I only have memories of you.

The once beautiful girl I knew,
made my life young and new,
she is now no longer in view.
I live my life in pain,
nevermore to return.

Baby Girl

It starts with your love,
a new beginning arrives,
a baby from heaven,
with stars in her eyes.

So precious and new,
can't take my eyes off of you,
so tender to the touch,
I want to hold her so much.

She's so tender and warm,
since the day she was born,
with hearts that are lite,
her future's so bright.

Time goes by and within a wink,
she's all grown up, pretty in pink,
now married and gone,
with babes in her arms.

I remember the day,
a babe in my arms,
so tender and new,
how I wish I had that back too.

Wedding Day

I saw her in the park one day.
Our eyes has met, our hearts had too.
We courted for a while,
before we said I do.

Her parents did not approve,
our love was too strong for them to disapprove.
They did not think kindly of me,
I had taken their little girl away with me.

The wedding day arrived,
she was so happy to be my bride,
our hearts were now one,
her old life was now done.

The voyage had started,
a new beginning was made.
With her by my side,
made my life stronger inside.
We learned as we live, with much more to give.

It was not long,
as two girls came along,
the love of our lives,
made us rich and alive.

As time went on,
our daughters were grown,
now married, they gave us a gift

that they own, five grandchildren,
whom we love and cherish,
a gift that was made in heaven.

Colors of the Rainbow

It takes sunshine and rain,
to make the rainbow appear.
Like the colors of the rainbow,
each color so pretty and so nice,
reflects the rainbows in my life.

Red, reflects the passion in my life,
the love I had for my wife.
Dreams we shared together,
which had lasted forever.

Orange, the sailor's storm in the sky,
for what tomorrow might bring.
The tempest sky may bring on the storm,
we need the rain to make the flowers bloom.
With each new flight, our rainbow grows.

Yellow which makes our hearts so lite,
our spirits are so right.
Like sunshine on a cloudy day,
we continued life, our way.

The springtime of green,
which made mountains and hills,
so quiet and siren.
Her green eyes sparkled and gleam,
love in her heart, that I dreamed.

Skies of blue that made her heart so true,
that was meant only for you.
Sometimes I have visions of life,
that was meant for a dream for another life,
when she was my wife.

Violet, the Color She Loved

The day we were wed,
brought tears to my eyes.
Walking down the aisle,
I saw the orchid she carried,
the day we were married.

The spectrum of colors in the rainbow,
we're tried-and-true.
They beam together,
like our lives were too.

Golden Years

No one knows how much I cry,
each and every day.
My days are long and lonely,
since you went away.

I wait for the pain to stop,
it gets more intense as days go by.
The more I think of you,
the more I need you; the more I cry.

I write these words of love,
to mend the wound within my heart,
but words will never mend a broken heart.

I cry alone without a tear,
like a well runs dry,
I'm all dried up inside.

I say tomorrow will be better,
that day never comes,
as each day is worse.
It's the same old verse.

I know now there's no cure for my wound.
I had my turn at life,
you only go around once,
there's no do-over in life.

There is no pain in life that I felt worse
than the pain of losing a wife,
all those many years of love and fun,
are over and done, getting older is no fun.

When you get old, they call it the golden years.
When you're alone, it's full of memories and tears.
Whoever penned that phony phrase,
must have been a script writer, with his mind in a haze.
You try to make the best of the time you have left,
you have a fake smile on your face, it's not your best.

I tell you in truth,
the golden years are in your youth,
give that scriptwriter a boot.

Old Feelings

I dreamed a dream of you last night,
I got that old feeling.
You were standing in a bright sunny light,
and when you came in sight,
I got that old feeling.
You were as beautiful as before,
when you came through the door.
My heart skipped a beat.
We held each other tight,
and the feeling felt so right.
Once again I got that old feeling.
We kissed as before.
I felt that old yearning,
deep inside me burning.
In a flash, it did not last.
I awakened from that dream,
with a smile on my face,
and once again I had that old feeling.
Others say, get a life,
play the game of life and get another.
I cannot play the game of life,
the feeling is not the same.
What is one expected to do?
My heart belongs to only you.

With all the years gone by,
you lose the loved one by your side,
you have an empty feeling deep inside.
You're alone in a world of despair,
a nobody, nobody cares.

All the money in the world does not help,
you can't buy happiness in the mall of despair.
No one can feel the anger you feel,
if the love that you had isn't real.

Peanut Butter and Jelly

They said we go together like peanut butter and jelly,
they called us the lovebirds,
our years of silver and gray.
We found the true meaning of love.
We were living in the Land of Oz,
a land of make believe come true.

Our hearts were together as one.
Though true love comes just once,
I'm so lucky we met and yet,
60 years went quickly you can bet.

Suddenly one day our years had ended,
her illness could not be mended.
with ten days left, our eyes had met
uncontrollable tears were wept.
Her hand held my face,
with a sweet kiss on the lips,
she said, I love you so, I'll never let you go.

It's been one year since she left,
the heartache never ends.
When I close my eyes to sleep each night,
I opened the door to paradise,
to see the love my eyes are longing for,
just as before, it does not happen anymore.

Man of the Year

(The tale of Jeff, my son-in-law)

He's the man for all seasons,
sweet as could be, the pick of the crop.
When you need a handyman,
that's when you call the candy man,
within a wink he will repair your sink.

Whatever you ask, he'll will never say no,
he'll try his best to give it a go.
Whatever the sport he knows it all,
he can argue with the best,
If you dare, you can give it a test.

He's the greatest Monday morning quarterback,
I ever knew. If you don't believe, just give him a review. Monday morning he
picks all the winners,
in football he'll say is vikes are the best,
other sports, he knows all the rest.

When Monday morning rolls around,
he's up bright and early, does not make a sound,
as his dog Luna's around.

Off he goes to work with coffee in hand.
His office is in the hall next to the john.
If he hears a sound, he'll be jumping around.
His desk is a box with papers scattered about.
With his stapler in hand, he now takes command.
He starts the day with a grin and a smile,

staples his way with all the papers around,
it doesn't take long when he's in command,

The next day, he's off again running,
bright and early to cut Pop's lawn.
He trims the hedges with vigor and haste,
as this man has no time to waste.

He saves a day for his mom,
to check on her to see if she's fine.
Help her in her needs,
she's so happy to see him indeed.

Weekend comes, work week is through,
there's always something to do.
Some time is free, watches TV.
Has a soft spot to see how my Giants may be.
To all the people he knows, he's held dear,
He is the man of the year.

Escape

It may seem strange to some,
I write these simple poems of love,
When the love I had was done.
My love for her was never thorough,
some may never have a clue.

Some would say, why?
When you lost the love that you had,
you bring heartache which is bad.
The inspiration to write these poems of love
brings me back to when our hearts were one.

The years went by too fast,
I write poems to make the memories last.
It was a Romeo and Juliet syndrome,
that was in our married life,
that made our love grow strong and bright.

Poems express my thoughts of love,
for the only love I ever had.
It brings sanity to my lonely days.
It's an escape of sort, in many ways.

Where only those who lost,
would know the burning feeling of that loss.
It is the life in which I dwell.
It is the life I call hell,
an empty soul in a shell.
There's no escape from grief.

It's a place where one goes to weep.

Heart full of anger and despair.

When the time comes for me, she'll be there.

Remembering Will Have to Do

The song that love birds sing,
the youth of endless spring,
the dreams of yesterday.
I'll remember till the day I die,
cannot be wiped away in days gone by.

When your hair turns to gray,
search the corners of your mind,
the happy days when she was mine.
The secrets we had, only she would know,
were like a Broadway show.

Young days of our lives we took for granted.
Now my mind is old and frantic.
Only memories will have to do,
I have dreams and tears thinking about you,

Will this river of tears never end?
Or will it pour into the ocean of my heart.
That will be the day when I depart.

Heart Full of Love

She left me with tears and sorrow,
on a journey far from home.
A place of peace and rest,
never more to roam.

Anger, grief, sweat, and tears,
are the norm of the day.
My life is but a dream,
a dream of yesterday.
The days we did things our way.

I fantasize the life we had.
We shared a life of hopes and dreams,
all of which came true.
Now my only thoughts are to follow you.

Alone with my shadow that follows me about.
I peer through my window, I see the sleet and snow about.
With a chill in the air and the darkness of night,
alone in my secret, I wonder if this could be the night.

My Heart Is a Lonely Place

My heart is a lonely place,
a place in which I dwell,
when there's no one to share,
to give you a welcome hand
makes you aware how much you really care.

The clouds hide a sunny day,
the acid rain from the skies above.
Each day a tempest sky that brow's a storm to come.
The winds which makes my heart a dancer,
nature's way to answer.

The morning sun brings another day,
that chase the storm away.
I see the shadow of her laughing face,
the face I used to embrace.

She made my life young and new,
my heart is now black and blue.
An empty place showing the signs of wear,
I'm still hoping she is there.

Where Are You?

Where have you gone without me?
Since you went away love,
what am I to do?
There is no the thrill without you, where are you?

Long walks along the waterway,
holding hands like teenagers in love.
I look around and don't know where to start.
I searched my soul to find a way but it's all in vain.

Where did you go in haste?
How can I go on without you?
Remembering will not do.
The sweet smell from your hair,
the essence of you is always there.

From where you are come take me by the hand,
let's fly away to distant shores.
If only for a little while, to see your smiling face.
I am only a heartbeat away from where you are.

I see your face in every flower,
your silence is an inspiration.
I wish upon a star, not far from where you are,
to see your smiling face watching over me.

Each day I look for a better way.
I cast around in the valley of my heart,
where I cherish all you gave me,
I remain in the darkness of my soul.
Where are you?

As Time Goes By

Time is the essence of all healing,
when you lose someone dear to you.
The wound you have is not revealing,
you still have that same old feeling.

As time goes by, the feeling is still there,
but nevertheless, the heartache makes you aware.
Time will never heal a broken heart.
It may mend your wound,
it cannot mend a broken heart.

Some poems were the sign of the times,
things that happened, as time goes by.
I end this book of love poems to show how much I care.
She was the center of my universe,
which can never be reversed.

IT WAS A MARRIAGE MADE IN HEAVEN
Harry Scrudato

We don't cry because it's over, we smile because it happened.